AF595043

HEALING AFTER MISCARRIAGE

Book of Poems

Vicki Renz

ISBN: 978-3-00-067484-6

Honouring the memory of five beautiful angels who gave me the inspiration and energy to create these poems

CONTENT

ACKNOWLEDGMENTS

I am thankful for the journey this life has taken me on. For the babies that I lost and the babies that I have. For the healing journey that miscarriage took me on; opening up doors that I never knew existed. For the healers who have taught me the many skills I have and use to help others today. For the mentors who have encouraged and supported me to speak my voice, to become the person I am today. To my husband for being part of this journey with me and giving me the time to create my book, website, YouTube channel and coaching programmes.

POEMS

I carried a soul and for some moments we were one,

But you left me and now within me

There's a space that feels so numb.

I miss you with all my might

Now that you belong to the stars in the night.

A heart with a piece that is missing.
Who were you going to be?
Unanswered questions.
I'll never get to know the answers,
That's why you are a piece of my heart that is missing.

The depth of my sadness,
The depth of my grief,
How can I begin to express
My feelings of disbelief?
How can anyone understand
The feelings I have beneath?
How is it possible that life goes on?
A moment in my belly, now gone.

Like a whisper of wind through the trees,
A bird singing beautifully,
Raindrops into water, sparkling and trickling downstream.
I am all of these.
Forever part of you eternally.
Keep your eyes open. Listen and look out for me.
The beauty of the world. There! That's me.

Angels are happy, angels smile,
They protect. They radiate light,
Feel my light, feel my protection,
Mummy, I am your angel now,
Listen for me on a starry night.

I am dancing,

I am over there.

Golden and soaring above you,

Above you in the air.

No one else can see you, but I know you are there,

I carried you, I felt you. Now you are somewhere in the air.

Flying free with the birds forever, please know I will always care.

I will always see you there, my free flying soul in the air.

I do not understand,
I never got to hold your hand
Or laugh with you and dance on the sand.
It hurts so much not having you here,
I promise I'll remember you, year after year.
I will always be your mummy forever,
One day we'll be again together.

Mummy, look up,

Can you see that smiling blue sky?

That's me mummy.

It's going to be ok. I am still here…

Just further away,

Watching you from up high.

My heart is heavy but I cannot cry,
All I can think of is „why, why, why?“
A feeling of emptiness that cannot be refilled,
Of not understanding life and the world.
I don’t want to be saying goodbye.
It wasn’t supposed to be this way, but I will try.
Try to acknowledge that you will no longer be
Physically here on the earth of me.
My baby, my love for you does not end here,
You are part of me forever, year after year.

I know that you are hurting.
Your heart is heavy and aches.
Now that I am gone,
Remember me, I'm your little one.
I am ok here, part of the stars and sun.

The rain that patters on the window pane,
Slowly sliding down and gathering in pools,
I sometimes feel like that one little drop,
Sliding down into deep sorrow pools.
But that pool of sorrow is not alone,
It is met and joined by many more drops,
Each growing together, building up,
Until suddenly they flow out together,
Into a future full of the vast unknown.

I pick up my sorrowful heart and warrior on,
Because it's not over, it's just begun.
I set my sorrow free to the wind and the sea,
And I stand, a warrior woman, my sword in my hand.

You will never be alone, that's the beauty of life…

I am a creation that lives on.

Life is infinite.

A loss that no one can see,
The only one feeling such grief is me.
How can anyone else possibly know
How it feels to carry but then have to let go?

Where did your soul go to?

Were you called away?

What made you leave so quickly?

I don't know what to say.

The plans I had for you and I,

They are no more, I had to say goodbye.

When the robin stops by and winks his eye,
I ask, „Is that you? Come to say hi? "
You give a little nod and whistle at me,
Look out for little signs, that's me, you will see.

Close to sunset, when the clouds have a golden tinge,
A gentle breeze brushes my cheek,
Or was it your wings?
The memory of you forever imprinted in me.
You belong in the sky now, flying forever free.

I am one amongst the stars in the night sky,
I am watching over you
My love forever twinkling when you look up high.
For a time, I was a special part of you.
Now part of something more immense,
Flying free with angel wings in the heavens.

I say goodbye to you my sweet dear soul,
Although you leave behind a gaping hole,
I know you weren't meant to be in this time and place,
I say goodbye with love as you float into space.
We are all made of stars and that's where you've gone.
Back to the place where life all began.
Goodbye my sweet angel, now go shine your light.
Keep sparkling over us all through the night.

AFFIRMATIONS

ABOUT AFFIRMATIONS

Positive thoughts send new instructions to your brain which help you to feel good.

Going through miscarriage is like being on a rollercoaster of emotions. We find ourselves questioning, blaming, getting angry, perhaps jealous. Feeling downright miserable and lost.

The healing journey is to allow yourself to get to a place of acceptance and forgiveness. Practicing affirmations on a daily basis can really help you to reach that place. Practice them upon waking and before going to sleep. Keep them around you so that you can read through them when you are feeling low.

I am worthy of being a mother

My body is perfectly healthy

I am a good and loving mother

I am a mother to an angel

I recognise you as an important part of my life journey

I am grateful for each morning I wake up

Each morning is a new chance

I can do this

I am worthy of being loved

I am worthy of feeling loved

I am grateful for our time together

I am grateful for the memories we made

I am your mother

I am eternally filled with love for you

I am forever receiving your love

YOUR NOTES

ABOUT THE AUTHOR

Vicki Renz, mother to two boys and recurrent miscarriage survivor, is founder and director of Oh My Mama Body, the specialist portal for women.

The empathy that exudes from Oh My Mama Body makes Vicki an honest source that thousands of women trust. After going through the traumatic experience of multiple miscarriages, Vicki embarked on a deep study of healing techniques.

Vicki mastered healing techniques and developed her unique Healing After Miscarriage coaching programme to help others with their journeys. Like a guiding light, Vicki coaches women through their journey from pain and grief through to acceptance and wholeness.

If you feel like you are caught up in a web of emotions, feeling like half the person you were before, like you are just trying to hold it together, visit Vicki's transformational coaching programme. Sometimes it just takes an outside perspective to open up the pathway to moving forward. Vicki understands the depth of your emotions and provides a pathway to move you through the cycle of grief to becoming whole and empowered again.

Follow the link below for all of Vicki's healing after miscarriage supportive resources:
https://ohmymamabody.com/healing-after-miscarriage/

www.ingramcontent.com/pod-product-compliance
Lightning Source LLC
LaVergne TN
LVHW070609170726
843515LV00004B/23